Lost on the Blood-Dark Sea

—

Robert Cooperman

FUTURECYCLE PRESS
www.futurecycle.org

Cover artwork, "Ulises y las Sirenas" by John William Waterhouse; cover and interior book design by Diane Kistner; Adobe Garamond text and titling

Library of Congress Control Number: 2019955464

Published by FutureCycle Press
Athens, GA, USA

ISBN 978-1-942371-94-6

For Beth, my Penelope, my everything

Contents

PROLOGUE

Odysseus Leaves Troy

We'll pull for Ithaca's cliff-crusted shore,
easy work now we're leaving Troy behind,
and joyously rid of ten years of war

that threatened to swallow us like a boar
grunting for acorns amid strangling vines.
Now, we're sailing off from Troy's fatal shore,

back to our precious homes; how our hearts soar
to be rid of wading through death's foul slime:
at last free of ten years of filthy war.

You'd think I was murderous to the core,
that I loved smashing heads and splitting spines,
impatient for foes on Ithaca's shore:

too placid, not enough glory and gore
to keep me busy; peace, a waste of time,
when I could be waging merciless war.

But oh, how these bleak years weighed more and more
on me, an impossible peak to climb.
Yes, now we're pulling for home's rocky shore,
Ithaca's cliffs like gold, after this war.

PART I

—

THE RAID ON THE CICONES

Xenios Finds a Way to Escape Troy

On an afternoon free of the endless
battles I've somehow escaped in one piece,
I search the strand, and come upon a dinghy,
and jump in, to sail to where there's no fighting,
and no bitch-Helen on Troy's ramparts, blowing
mocking kisses, as if our sole purpose
was to be killed for her entertainment.

For as many years as I can count on
the fingers of my two hands—lucky not
to have lost any from the Trojans' swords—
I've served Odysseus, a good master,
but this war will last 'til not a man's alive.

I raise the sail and work the tiller. She
skims across open water: the sail
snapping like the songs of morning birds,
as Ilium grows small and disappears,
and my jolly dinghy canters toward
whatever harbor she may take me to.

I pray for a deserted coast: no one
to fall out with, over a slut like Helen.
Though if there's one woman on this otherwise
empty shore I sail to, and she's passable
looking, with half her teeth, and her breasts don't
sag too much, and we can work as a team,

it'll feel like I've been saved from Hades
and wafted to the one Elysium
us poor working bastards will ever know.

The Myrmidon Letheres, a Stowaway on Odysseus' Flagship

With Lord Achilles killed, his crazed bastard
Neoptolemus grabbed our spoils, claiming
Troy indestructible without his sword,
and left us—who had fought ten years—nothing.
I'd no wife, children; my parents dead: all
I had to look forward to, endless toil
in Neoptolemus' fields, tossed hard
bread and moldy cheese until I'd have dropped.
So I hid on Odysseus' flagship,
knowing him for a fair and true leader.

When I popped out of hiding, we had put
Troy leagues behind us. Odysseus smiled,
"Well done, whoever you might prove to be."
That's when the storm reared up: giant clouds black
as mad Neoptolemus' brow when any
dared speak against him, rage springing from him
like a pack slashing at a wounded stag.

Odysseus' men grumbled I'd brought
this ill-luck, thus should be flung overboard
to appease the Sea Lord, Poseidon.

"Row!" he roared. "This storm is no more his fault
than slut-Helen's yapping little lap dog."
So we all put our backs into our oars;
my new lord taking his place: his example
giving us strength; finally, the wind calmed,
and we spied a wide, welcoming harbor.

My Lord Odysseus took me aside.
"I can sense what brought you to seek shelter
on my ship, and you did good work today.
So I'll give you a portion of my spoils.
You'll find Ithaca more pleasant than the land
Neoptolemus lashed you to row for.

Elpenor, Rowing Away from Troy, Under Odysseus' Command

Arrogant, headstrong, too damn sure of himself;
of course, but he knew all our names, the names
of our wives and children, recalled each man
who fell, every one of our wounds, offered
wine, a joke, words of encouragement, shared
our winter-meager outdoor fires, and didn't
loll in a warm tent with warmer slave girls.

Agamemnon? He treated underlings
like sheep for slaughter: drove his chariot
over their corpses if it meant getting
at booty he'd strip off dead enemies,
or one of his own allies, if their arms
dazzled: greedier than a snarling jackal.
Not that Odysseus didn't toss us
shattered scraps sometimes, by way of tribute.
But often he took nothing, let us strip
corpses of finery like swarming ants.

He wept with us for home, never slapped us,
or called us cowards, unlike the other kings:
forever finding fault, no matter how well
vassals served and lost their one priceless life.
Nobles' noses in the air at our stink,
as if we hadn't lived rough for ten years.

But now we're rowing for sweet Ithaca;
I can smell her seaweed, can taste my wife's
lamb stews, onions bobbing in the thick broth
like tiny ships in a young prince's bath.
Still, something hisses in my troubled head,
some portent that the gods will fling hardships,
as if we've not endured enough of them.

But Odysseus soothes, "Don't think, just row."

Odysseus Surveys the Harbor of the Cicones

It looks like a fat island: sheep, goats, kine;
and from the crow's nest, I can make out grapes
so ripe they lie like panting, farrowing swine:
made to be raided by war-hardened men.
Besides, I have ten crowded ships to keep
in meat and wine for the long voyage back
to Ithaca, and no telling if the winds
will stay kindly behind us, or set us
spinning like children's tops about to topple.

So I give the order to attack: men
leap over the gunwales and charge the strand,
me in the lead, thrusting my sword left and right.
A swift raid, then we'll be plumping our sails
again, before the bumpkins see who hit them;
and if one or two plead to know—before
the great darkness takes them—who destroyed
their smug peace, I'll thump my chest and bellow:

"Odysseus, returning from victory
at Troy, to grab glory and honor, and make
every fat island between Ilium
and Ithaca quake at the snap of my sails,
the whistle of my true-flying arrows,
and the might of my armed comrades' strong swords."

Meliades, Dying at the Hands of the Cicones, on Ismarus

We're fighters, raiders; what we did at Troy,
and here on Ismarus: dividing spoils,
using their wives and daughters for our pleasure,
owed that for Troy's ten years of Tartarus.

So when Odysseus ordered us to
our boats, we shot back that here was plenty
of meat, wine, and soft women to enjoy
before sailing on. Who knew what hardships
awaited us at sea or on hostile coasts?

"Fools!" he thundered, slapped us with his sword-flat,
but none of us were budging: too tired,
too eager to stuff ourselves with roast meat,
to drink, and shove our poles in Ciconian
women, who cursed us, "Wait 'til our men return."
"They're dead," I taunted, "rotting in Hades!"

They came at us out of the East, at dawn,
a force gathered by the few survivors.
All day we fought, but at dusk we cracked.
Odysseus ordered us into our boats;
for once, we listened, but an arrow pinned me
to the ground; I was left bleeding, to die.
While writhing in pain, I started to laugh.

"You find torture amusing?" they demanded.

"It's just," I gasped, "that I made it through ten
long years at Troy, famous for its fighters,
only to die on this fucking shit-heap."
As I had hoped, their fury killed me quickly,
though I wander without coin on Styx's shore.
Home? I can barely recall Ithaca
and the drudgery of my shepherd life.

Lykanos, Rowing Safely Away from the Coast of Ismarus

Fucking Ismarians, pretending they'd never
launched a raid, never scraped marauder ships
onto others' strands, winged arrows at throats
before lookouts blew alarms, never drove spears
or swords into stomachs, never raped jades
or dashed infants' brains against stone walls,
never pillaged gold or silver or bronze,
never stole red cattle, pigs, goats, and sheep,
drained wine sacks, then rowed away, laughing.

Our world's one fast law? Raid or be raided,
as natural as wolves feeding on sheep,
as shepherds hunting packs mad on the blood
and bleats of helpless flocks. Thus men grow rich,
though Ismarians whined the gods were outraged.
The one outrage: we didn't load our ships
and row quickly away for Ithaca.
If we'd just listened to Odysseus,
we'd have left before their counterattack.

Instead, we mourn as we row: every boat
losing at least one good man, a stalwart
in battle; or campfire teller of tales;
an expert at roasting meat we'd lifted
from another encampment: the dull sods
not paying attention, Odysseus
scolding our theft from allies, but we saw
he was pleased—a father teaching his sons well.

Just let those Ciconians try revenge;
we'll lure them into a trap and kill every
last one of those puling little hypocrites.

Temnios Escapes the Land of the Cicones

Despite ten years of fighting, we're farmers,
tenders of livestock. We labored in vineyards,
joyously danced to crush grapes into wine.
But then dread Agamemnon's agents forced us
into his army, like funneling sheep
into a cote, easier to shear them,
to slit their fat throats in a narrow space.

And suddenly, we were adept with arms,
though we used pikes only to ward off wolves.
And the ash bow? My arms shook when I tried
to draw it back and let an arrow fly.
How I survived ten years of shitting myself
in terror I've no idea; I dreaded each battle,
hung back, unloosed a spear from time to time,
and sat silent by dusk fires, so men thought,

"Here's one who lets his deeds talk, not his mouth."
That plan worked, and I sailed home with my lord,
loving the tug of the sea on my oar,
'til he ordered us to attack Ismarus,
our ships already groaning with booty,
as if we'd stuffed ourselves in a great hall.

I was the one man with Odysseus
when he ordered us to leave with our loot.
But no, the rest would loiter, tempt the few
escaping Ciconians to gather
a force of allies; and of course they did.

Now we row for our lives, leaving comrades
and brothers dead upon Ismarus' strand.
Pray the gods, we'll head straight for Ithaca.
I've had enough adventures, want only
to wed, gallop children on my stout knees;
and if they ask about Troy, I'll tell them
I performed my duty, and nothing more.

Rhenon, Failing To Escape, After the Raid on the Cicones

Even after we stripped Troy like locusts
turning a fig orchard into a field
dead as Hades, we were wild for more loot,
so raided fat-for-the-plucking Ismarus.

After we'd stuffed the hulls of our wolf ships,
Odysseus warned we'd better sail off,
but we shouted him down, after ten years
of watching Agamemnon take his fill
and leaving us booty's bones and gristle.

So we feasted and fucked the night away,
but at sunrise, Odysseus sounded
the alarm: the Cicones had summoned their allies
in the night, their war cries terrifying.
Fleeing, I fell, my head striking a stone.

Coming to, I saw I'd been hauled to their town
and tied to a stake in their agora
'til the Sun's golden steeds raced above me,
my throat one great flame, as if I'd been forced
to drink a whole urn stinking with boar piss.

No one spoke: their silence more frightening
than the Furies' screams; the cries of Harpies.
At last, their leader proclaimed with a smile,

"You and your mates thought we'd make easy pickings,
that we'd offer no resistance to you
Achaeans, masters of the land and sea."

"Make me your slave," I begged. "Set me to work
on the hardest, dirtiest tasks you have."

But their headman set fire to the piled kindling:
smoke choking, flames licking like hungry hounds,
while brats danced to the music of my screams.

Rowing from the Coast of Ismarus, Thosos Mourns His Brother

Ten years we fought side by side: bull-steady.
But after this raid that killed my brother,
I ship my oar and weep: Kosos had but
to glance and know my mind, as I knew his;
he took the punishments I should've suffered,
and I the same for him; saved me from a boar
as I tossed him from the fangs of a bear.

But I couldn't save him from barbarous
Ciconians who counterattacked at dawn,
after we'd sacked their city, drank their wine,
ate their meat, and fucked their women senseless;
I'll never see him on this side of Hades,
and maybe not even there: I'd no chance
to leave the Ferryman's coin for Kosos'
passage past dread Styx to Elysium.

Even if we meet there, he'll not know me,
for once a man has crossed over, he forgets
all he knew and loved in this brief world above.
So, while I was useless in grief's talons,
Odysseus sat beside me, and soothed,

"We will mourn him, but first we all must row,
or the Ciconians will launch their ships.
It will do poor Tremnos no good if we can't
perform the rite to give him peace and rest.
So Thosos, my shipmate, row, for our lives
rely on your strong back and battle-wiry arms;
soon we'll make landfall, and pray for his soul."

How the man could weave word-spells of solace
to stop my tears, though I began to wonder
what I could say to my brother's widow,
and, worse, to our parents, if they hadn't
passed into the land of silence and shadows.

Mises, Thirteen Years Old, Escapes Odysseus' Raid
on the Cicones

When Father saw the first of their wolf ships
grind up our sand beach, he shoved me and hissed,
"Warn the others on our island's far coast!"
He grunted, an arrow piercing his chest;
crying, I ran as if wolves pursued me.
Finally, I gasped into the village.

"Stay here," the leader roared, but how could I,
when I had to see if Mother was alive,
and Stellios, and his older sister.
I spied her one time, in a mountain pond.
She'd gestured for me to join her, my head
spinning; her lips brushed my face; the world roared;
she laughed, my brow on fire with my soiled belly.
"Look," she cooed and pointed, "you're a man now."

Now, I run back to our hamlet; our women
tormenting injured raiders, and quickly
giving the blade of rest to our own wounded.
Fearful as a deer stepping into a glade,
I enter our hut: Mother a blood-poppet.
"I'll kill every last one of them!" I scream.

Then I stagger to Stellios' hut;
he's staring at his beautiful sister.
Sobbing, I help him lay her on the pyre
along with poor Mother and all the rest;
the priest lights the anointed pile and chants
to guide our dead to the Beautiful Land.

The Argives? We'd have left them for the dogs,
but they begin to stink; we bury them
without prayers or the Ferryman's coins
and swear never to speak of them again.

PART II

—

AMONG THE LOTOS EATERS

Odysseus Spots the Land of the Lotos-Eaters

When we spied the tauntingly gentle shore
of the Cicones, my men were too fed up
with the toils and blood-filthy coils of war—
still mourning the brothers and companions
they'd lost before Troy's implacable gates,
the years we'd been deprived of our dear homes
on rocky Ithaca, and dearer wives—
to listen to my commands to escape
with our easy booty, and the pleasure
of enjoying Ciconian women.

"We will stay here!" they all murmured, muttered,
angry as a hive disturbed by brash bears.

Disaster to linger overnight, but
my men had to find that out the hard way,
when the Ciconians and their allies
attacked at dawn; we fought, but finally
had to retreat to our ships and put backs
and arms into our oars as if running
from a bull that boys torment in its paddock.

Finally, I spot this misty strand, fog
hanging low as an Asian silk curtain;
I send a scouting party to determine
if the locals are hostile. Anything but,
the report comes back, but disconcerting
that only two men return to our ships.

The others, they say, have joined the natives,
seemingly satisfied with their sojourn
and delighting in the local vegetable.

"We will retrieve them, and find provisions
and drink here. But be watchful, and refuse
the herb if they offer it," I order,
then make our way up the strand, swords unsheathed.

The Lotos Eaters Complain About the Presence of Odysseus and His Shipmates

Like all mortals, they overindulge, eat
so much of the sacred plant they collapse
onto our laps and snort the laughter of boors;
thus disturb our rest, invade our soothing dreams
of soft waves; of combing goddess' tresses
before we make languorous love to them.

Worse yet, these louts trample the holy plants,
so ruin future crops, then burst into tears
and demand forgiveness, shove dagger hafts
at our spongy hands: justice too much effort.
Worst of all is their shouts to serving maids
to bring more and more, as if our supply were
inexhaustible as Zeus's ambrosia.

Their leader, Odysseus, recounts his exploits
as if we care this Troy was once a wonder
that these creatures helped reduce to rubble.
Always their way: first, they see something lovely;
then, all they can think is how to wreck it.

We close weary eyes, try to shut our ears,
breathe deeply of the peace we remembered
before their wolf ships scraped across our strand.

"Take your tales," we tell them, "of war's glory,
of contending with monsters, of heroes' quests.
Take them all; leave us our dreams of grass waving
like the sea when breezes riffle its surface,
of maids with kisses sweet as berry juice.

"Surely," we hiss, "your women and children
wait, fretting for your return. Go to them
and leave us, leave us, leave us—in peace."

Menardes Remains Among the Lotos Eaters

The others were dragged onto our long ships,
though they wept and kicked like snot-slimed brats
who rage against their nurses at bedtime.
I hid, and no one thought to look for me.

"But what of home?" one Lotos Eater asks.

"Home?" I mutter through moly's gentle haze.
"Home is a wife who has surely taken
a new man who'd kill me if I returned.
Home is children—and who knows how many
are mine—who've long ago forgotten me.

"Home was merciless Ithaca: each day
a battle to yank meager crops from fields,
and make sure cannibal sows didn't feast
on their young before we could fatten them
for Lord Odysseus' grand table.
Home is paying endless tax, and for what?
The privilege of following my Lord to Troy,
where so many of my comrades were slaughtered

"Home is a long, long journey away.
I'm here now, and here I will remain,
no fear of dying from crazed enemies,
nor shattering surf or ravenous monsters."

And even if the Lotos Eaters tire
of my presence, I spied a quiet cove
where I can eat moly and dream such dreams
a man sighs to reclaim, once he's awake.

Licius Remains Among the Lotos Eaters

I wandered off, and fell asleep inside
a cave, and was forgotten; when I woke
our last ships were vanishing for Ithaca.
I sat down and tore my hair and garments
and wept and wept for having lost my chance
to return home, to my wife and children.

I paced the strand, refused the Lethe-weed,
even when splendidly languorous maids
offered it, along with half-naked breasts,
though I confess I've succumbed to their charms:
one in particular, who's forgotten
the world less than the rest; she comforts me
when I sob of the far-off Ithaca
my shipmates must have fetched up at by now,
welcomed home by wives and their grown children.

So I light signal fires, but we're so far
from regular trade routes, the only reason
we made shore here was the thrashing storm winds.
But I'm building a raft: soon, I'll be ready
to sail for Ithaca, though this Lotos-maid's
lovely as our dreams of goddess Helen:
what kept us alive and hopeful at Troy,
more than tame thoughts for our faithful women
as the long years dragged on and on and on.

But I'll soon make amends to my dear wife,
though this maiden gives me such solace
I sometimes forget what tasks I must still
complete, for the voyage to Ithaca.

PART III

—

IN THE CAVE OF CYCLOPS

Cowering in Polyphemus' Cave, Meres Remembers His Brother,
Axatilles, the First Ithacan Killed at Troy

I'd warned him to crouch like the rest of us,
the Trojans banging swords against their shields,
our landing obvious to a blind man.
He rushed up the beach, as his wife and I
had sweated into each other in secret.
He'd never breathed a word. But, oh, his looks!

When the war ended at last, I could breathe
for the first time in years: a short sail home,
I thought, to Ithaca, and Basilla and me
telling our child who his real father was,
and performing rites to secure forgiveness.
But I cringe in this cave that stinks of sheep
and old cheese, and the death that'll devour me
in the grinding jaws of this giant monster
who tosses us down his maw like ripe grapes.

Better, I think, to have perished quickly
with Axatilles on that blood-smudged beach:
then the ferry ride to Elysium,
where I could've explained our lust to him;
so I wonder if this isn't the vengeance
Axatilles has spun from his black web
in the Land of Shades, though the dead are said
to forget us in their dark world of mists.

Brother, forgive me for taking your wife;
we were weak. But I fear we'll never meet,
and I'll wander forever, unforgiven.

Lethereus with Odysseus, after the Cave of the Cyclops

"My Lord, please," we begged our captain, "for love
of our homes, wives, and children we've not seen
in ten years, let's take these cheeses, these lambs,
and row from this monster's cavern as quick
as eagles with the flapping trout they've snatched."
But he was keen to win gifts from "our host."
Of course, the moment the monster returned
everything went to Hades faster than
when the Trojans launched poisoned darts at us:

Polyphemus grabbed two screaming comrades
and rammed them into his maw like raisins.
The rest of us scattered like farmyard hens,
while Odysseus stood, and gave the beast
his sacks of undiluted wine, winking
at us the fiend would soon be snoring.

All right, I'll give Odysseus this much,
his plan worked: the brute drunkenly asleep,
we sharpened a stake and poked out his eye
that bubbled like blood soup in a cauldron.
The creature howled, but felt the need to let
his sheep out to graze, and Odysseus
strapped us to their undersides, and followed.

But even as we scrambled for our ships,
our leader, our oh so clever leader,
couldn't resist taunting, so the giant
heaved blind boulders, and almost capsized us,
Odysseus roaring for us to row
as if pursued by merciless Furies.

Afterwards, while we wept for lost comrades,
he still raved and shook fists at the Cyclops:
polluting sacred hospitality,
so that I wondered who were the wise men
and who the dolt, though never so foolish
to ever utter those complaints out loud.

Dalos, Trapped in the Cave of Cyclops

When Odysseus coaxed the others out
to elude the Cyclops' fingers groping
to crush them like lice, I was too frightened
to move; my captain frowned and ran to leave,
Polyphemus howling for its lost eye.

But when it stumbled out—its dead eye smoking
from the sharpened stake Odysseus tempered—
I crept out, and prayed to scurry between
the Cyclops' legs thick as pine-tree stumps.
But at the sight of it—screaming, heaving
boulders into the sea—I froze again.

In that instant, a kinswoman of the brute
scooped me up; all went black as Tartarus.
I woke inside a cage, like those at Troy,
where a bird's melody was most welcome.

"Don't be afraid," she whispered. "I won't let
anything grab you, though Uncle would like
to eat you, to avenge his smoldering eye."
Then, like a mother-wolf, she chewed some meat,
and spat the mess out. Choking, I took some.
She stroked my trembling back with a finger,
cooed as if to a baby she was gentling
to sleep; my dreams woke me; my waking worse:
Polyphemus roaring like a great bear.

"Give it to me, whore, or I'll kill you too!"
But her club battered the side of his head,
and she dragged him out; I prayed she'd not tire
of me, so when she returned I murmured
a tune I'd heard as a child, made up words;
she smiled; when I finished, she commanded,
"Another!" I sighed; more words came to me
in this songbird-cage I'll never escape.

Styrones, Trapped in the Cave of the Cyclops

Here we are, trapped like rats by nasty boys,
except it's this huge booby of a monster
who thinks he'll eat us like plucked summer figs.

Odysseus, our captain, has this plan—
now that he's blinded the murderous oaf
who bellows and blunders about his cave—
to wait until the Cyclops' sheep need
to be let out, so they can feed, piss, shit,
and fuck to their baa-ing hearts' content.
Our leader will tie us to their bellies
as they trot past the brute, to gain our freedom.

I've got a better plan: if we wait
until the Cyclops has staggered right up
against the stone he set at the entrance
to keep us trapped here, I'll hurl my javelin
at his throat; he'll stagger against the boulder
and knock it out of place; then we'll swarm him
with swords, and skip away, without having
to worry he'll fumble around woolly
bellies with fingers thick as the trunks of pines.

Plus, we can take our fill of his food stores,
leisurely as women bargaining with
a peddler in their great halls, then sail home.

Does our Captain expect men terrified
not to shriek while grubby fingers dash them
against cave walls? My way a direct assault,
no sly subterfuge that might turn on us,
as a boar will lunge at its attackers.
My blood shrills like a falcon to kill him,
and kill him and kill him and kill him again.

Leonides, Bard of Ithaca, Escapes the Cyclops

At Troy, I watched the fighting from a poet's
safe distance, then composed my battle songs,
always chanting Odysseus' feats,
as well as the deeds of fellow Achaeans;
lauding Agamemnon, who swelled to hear
himself honored when I'd enhance his deeds.
But in truth, he never drove into battle
unless accompanied by outriders
as his shields: their duty to die for him.

My Lord Odysseus, the true hero:
for the men he slew; plus, sneaking behind
Trojan lines to ferret out battle plans;
and most important, coaxing other lords
to build the Horse, to end the war at last.

Joyous to sail for Ithaca, for home,
thinking the voyage would take a soft week
of following breezes and steady oars,
while I encouraged the lads with my songs.

But it's one horror after another;
I fear none of us will reach Ithaca.

Still, my voice and plucking fingers, my weapons
against despair, though each strange creak and groan
swivels me in my seat on our flagship:
fearful something huge will devour us.
Yet I manage to form words and strum my lyre
like a cunning spider, while scouring coasts
for landmarks that mean journey's welcome end.

Sailing from the Cyclops, Odysseus Apologizes to His Crew

Forgive me, my dear shipmates, but our years
of fighting, killing, and dying at Troy,
and the leagues and leagues we've sailed trying
to find home drove me into Discord's maw.
You're right, I should have led us away
from the monster's cave before he returned.

I forgot there are forces and creatures
under Lord Zeus' treacherously blue sky
that can kill us all in a blinked instant,
without a care how cunning a man is.

I played with the lives of shipmates, and lost,
or rather, they lost because of my hubris,
my desire to be lauded as Troy's slayer,
while, to much of the world Troy doesn't exist.
I have made too much of myself, and thought
Polyphemus should bend to my shrewdness.

So let us put our backs into our oars
and pull for home; with luck, a week of rowing.
One more port of call, at the God of the Winds,
then the welcome cliffs of hard Ithaca,
and our wives running for our arms; our sons
shaking hands like well-met brothers; our daughters'
darling bairns bouncing for joy on our knees.

A little more patience, my dear comrades,
and all our journeying will be over.

Odysseus, After His Apology to His Crew

What came over me? Maybe I'm weary
of being the sober leader who must
be watchful, who must rein in my crewmen
as if infants with no sense that to touch
flames is to burn. Just as much, I wanted
tribute, honors from the monster, and also
to have him acknowledge that great No Man
is a king to be lauded by all the world.

I knew if I didn't apologize,
my men would mutiny, and though I might
talk my way out of their rage, I might not,
and if they were of a mind to oust me,
none would live to see Ithaca.

At Troy, we knew who the enemy was,
but we've wandered into a sea of terror,
so I pull at the oars, and make them sing,
to keep their hearts from stopping in terror.

I grip my tattered shield of confidence,
or my men will lose hope; then where will we be?

PART IV

—

OF WINDS AND CANNIBALS

Polymenes Opens the Bag of Winds to Disastrous Consequences

Ten years I battled at Troy, and for what?
A pittance of Odysseus' booty.
So when Aeolus, god of the winds, gave
our captain-king that heavy sack, I thought—
as did the others—here was more treasure.
Indeed, he kept it firmly between his feet
at the tiller while we rested on our oars
and let the breeze bear us to Ithaca.
So as my comrades' elbows dug at my sides,
and Odysseus, for once, snored and slept,
I opened the sack, expecting gold, gems.

Instead, all the winds of the world leapt out:
the storm batting us: a lynx with a hare.
If only Odysseus had told us
its contents! But as always, he adored
his secrets, his cleverness, more than us,
who'd fought far from Ithaca's turquoise skies.
All night and day we reefed the sails and bailed.
Finally, the storm blew its fury out,
and we fetched up outside a calm harbor,
the shore inviting as our wives' warm arms.

Our other ships dropped anchor in the cove,
but Odysseus held back, the coward,
trying to make us think he senses danger,
while our comrades feasted on luscious fruit,
and I screamed, "We're starving; enter the cove!"

"Hard astern!" he shouted. I look: monsters
feasting on our brothers like fresh baked loaves,
Odysseus staring bronze darts at me.
Not as if I acted alone, but always
the blame falls on me, like a heaved boulder.
As for our poor shipmates who perished here,
who's to say they're not the fortunate ones—
our voyage to Ithaca without end.

Straygos, As They Drop Anchor Outside the Harbor of the Laestrygons

I didn't spend ten years at Troy, losing
an eye in one battle, to learn nothing
from Odysseus: if a harbor looks
too calm, you can bet just beyond the shore
trouble's boiling like Medea's cauldron.

Even before I voiced my fears, our lord
dropped the sea anchor, and we rode the waves
beyond this cove, tempting as a whore's breasts.
But that loudmouth Polymenes, who'd slashed
open the god's sack of winds, thinking gems
glittered inside—shouted, "Follow the others!"

Had Odysseus but nodded his head,
I'd have slit his throat faster than a ham.
But my captain graciously let him rant,
'til we gasped at the shore's ravenous monsters.

"Row, row!" that fool Polymenes shrieks now;
I cuff him, shove an oar into his hands,
the rest of us finding a swift rhythm.

As we row, we can't help but watch our mates
being torn apart and eaten by beasts
more misshapen than the stuff of nightmares,
which I know are prophecies: none of us,
save Odysseus, will see home again.
This I've seen in dreams: my end, at least, free
of pain, unlike our comrades, at the claws
of those creatures we frantically row from.

Xanthos Considers His Friend Polymenes, as They Row Away
from the Land of the Laestrygons

Every man in our nine other ships killed
by those monsters, and all Polymenes
can think of is that their hardships are done.
And still he mutters against our captain,
Odysseus, for withholding the bag
of the winds from us, keeping its contents
secret, when time and again, he's saved us
from danger with his strength and cleverness:
seeing threats the rest of us are blind to—
blithe as lambs that can't feel the shepherd's blade.

Always Polymenes complains, blames others
for his own failings, and yet I loved him.
But no more: let him survive on his wits
and stop whining; not his place to protest
his share of the spoils. We all had fair shares,
but he'd never admit that; all of it
too little, but who'd he complain to then?

And to shed not a tear for the good men
his foolhardy opening of the god's
sack of winds caused! The war has tainted him.
When…if we do find Ithaca, I fear
for my poor sister, his wife. The least thing
wrong, he'll be a leopard at her throat.
She'll run to me, Xanthippe and my wife
never getting on, so my life will be
worse than Ixion on his wheel of flames.

But we face more pressing problems: reduced
to one ship, we're prey for monsters and witches
and row with hearts grieving for our lost friends
and kin; all, that is, save Polymenes.

Memnes, Attacked by the Laestrygons

Nine of our ships ventured into the harbor;
only Odysseus held back; we others
saw fruit trees in succulent abundance,
and signaled to our captain. But he kept
a tight rein, as if restraining a stallion
that will need stamina for a long race.

When the monsters showed themselves, we ran,
but the creatures hurled stones at our vessels;
our one desperate chance: to hope the beasts
made quick work of us, so huge, our weapons
useless as ants battling boys who crush armies;
and each monster is faster than swift Achilles
when he toyed with fleeing, craven Hector.

Now, I'm the one man still alive, the beasts
edging in, not for fear of my sharp sword—
little better than a bronze pin against
their leathery hides—but curious to see
what sort of strange, wee creature I might be.
Their leader brings me to his face, his maw
wide as the cave-mouth of monster-Cyclops,
his fangs wolf-yellow, huge as cedar trees.

My fists flail; the beast laughs and flicks me off
like a bug. I hit the water, like landing
head-first on a deck, falling from the mast,
like one mate, his blood an urn of spilled dye.
At least no pain, as I drift down and down,
lay sprawled beside Styx without the coin
for the Ferryman in this twilight.
What's another eternity of waiting
when, at worst, I can be killed only once?

PART V

—

WITH BEASTS AND WITCHES

Partaxes Escapes Circe's Cave

How did I survive ten years at Troy?
I never tried to go against fighters
like Aeneas, Sarpedon, or Hector;
always chose lesser men; picked off stragglers
as wolves bring down the lame in a fleeing herd.

Now, with these witchy maids inviting us
into their dimly lit cave, I hang back:
suspicious, smelling something not quite right;
maybe it's that these women, Queen Circe
especially, are avid as old hags
slavering to make a meal of small boys;
or that there are far too many fawning
creatures with the lost look of doomed men.

The others rush in, men deprived of women
for too long; even Chief Odysseus
casts aside caution like a tattered cloak.

Now, when I behold Circe strike her wand
and transform my shipmates into creatures,
I run for the harbor, find a dinghy
I hope contains magic in its sails
to take me straight to blessed Ithaca.

But even if I drown, it's a better fate
than the one that awaits Odysseus
and his crew at the hands, and fangs, of Circe
and her band of pitiless man-eaters.

Elpenor Falls off the Roof of Circe's Palace
and Winds Up in Hades

Lying poets will proclaim that I got drunk
and fell off the roof: a shirker deserving
to wander Hades' shore clamorous
with other rogues short the Ferryman's coin.

The true tale? The air inside the Witch's lair
cloying as a sea of honey. I sat
on the roof, one of Circe's maids nestled
down: a vixen shape-shifter to remind
me of my dear, lost wife; so when the slut

climbed atop me, her hair whipping frenzies,
I thought my luck burned bright as the far stars,
as full as the moon. She shoved me; my skull
cracking like an egg on the stony ground;
next thing I knew, I was begging a ride
across grim Styx from Charon, who shouted,

"The coin! I'll not let beggars board my boat."

Curse the swine, but still my fate's preferable
to Odysseus': for I can hide
under some canvas on Charon's ferry,
and fool him into rowing me across,
then leap onto the dear, far shore and taunt,

"See where your stupid greed has gotten you!"

I'll find a flock of sweet and eager maidens
to enjoy blissful Elysium with;
and, when I flag, I'll compose my epic.

*Aglaia, One of Circe's Handmaidens, Considers Her Mistress
and Odysseus' Crew*

Every time a crew wanders onto our shore,
Lady Circe feeds and entertains them,
then turns them into sheep, goats, and the swine
we feast on, or keep as pets, their sad eyes
pleading to be returned to their former states.

"We merely make them what they already are,"
she smirks when we ask why we must do this.
But when this Odysseus and his mates
stumbled up our strand, one lost mariner
tugged at me with his sad, sea-weary eyes,
and for being deprived of his dear wife.

"Who's to say she hasn't taken up with
some younger, stronger man, who'll slaughter me?"

"If you like," I spoke softly, "we can look
into my crystal, to detect her heart."
He shook his head, afraid to face his fate.
"Am I not pleasing?" I lay on the sand.

"Oh, lovelier even than Queen Helen,"
he swore and sobbed, then lay down beside me.

"You must leave this place," I whispered at dawn,
"or My Lady will turn you into a beast.
Steal a dinghy, raise its sail, and row far
and fast; and a steadfast breeze home to you."

Standing on the strand, I watched 'til his sail
disappeared, then turned to find My Lady.
"What a little fool you are, to believe him."

"I know," I smiled, "but, just this once, pleasant
to grant a mortal mercy; their lives are short
and vicious. No harm to cede him a night
of glory, even if his wife's truer
than he has a right to expect of her."

Selax, Turned Into a Leopard by Circe

At first, I pleaded in my strange new voice
that roared so fiercely it terrified me.
Too, I shrank from being fed some shipmates
transformed into swine: their cries pitiful
before they were bled, the meat tossed to me.

But I got used to the fare, accustomed
to no longer being a man, but a beast
with a roar that made lesser beasts panic.
Best, Circe and her handmaids would shape-shift,
the witch a black panther so sleek I'd lick
her fur, so she'd purr, before we mated.

Why I wanted to be a man again
I've forgotten, now that shipmates set sail.
No, far better to remain a great cat.
Let the others sail off to certain doom;

I'll lie beside Circe: the fire, star-dancing;
then, she'll call on her maidens to bathe her
in milk, then change into that black panther;
and we'll cavort, then listen to her nymphs
play upon golden lyres and make up tales—

some about Troy—so a tear might trickle
down my snout. But I'll forget those lost years
and purr at the beauty of the plucked tunes,
the music of the words that have nothing
to do with me or whatever I once was.

PART VI

—

IN THE LAND OF THE DEAD

Praxiles Follows Odysseus Down to the Land of the Dead

I was desperate to talk to and hold Mother—
as she'd held me as a child—one last time,
though I feared I'd be joining her too soon,
the way our mariners' luck was running
away like panicked chariot horses
on this eternal voyage to Ithaca
that had already cost us all but one
of our ships and most of my companions.

I'd left Mother on her deathbed; barely
time to hold her hand, kiss her parchment-dry
face, to hear her final blessing, before
I was hauled away to impatient Troy.

Still, I had to see her, hear her voice,
soft as fragrant pines on warm spring evenings.
The dead can speak only if they drink blood;
like my captain, I brought a wine sackful
and kept well back in that shade-haunted realm.

Now, as I trailed him to the dark kingdom,
not once did he command me to turn back—
not that I'd have heeded him. I watched him
consult with Tiresias, but could hear
not a word: just as well, since I could feel
in my bones—grown cold and creaky—that none
of us would ever see Ithaca again.

Once Odysseus finished, I poured wine
on the ground, waited for Mother to speak
a word or two. But though other shades tried
to drink and ask about the world above,
and I slapped them with my sword flat, Mother
never appeared to make me think, somehow,
she had survived her rasping breaths that stabbed
her lungs and my sobbing heart, to give me hope:
maybe the most dangerous foe of all.

Odysseus, After His Visit to Hades

After Tiresias foretold the dangers
yet lurking on our voyage home, I spied
Mother and tried to embrace her: a mist
that, had I met her in the world above,
I'd have dismissed as a trick of the fog.

But here, a ghost forced to lap like a hound,
from the pool of blood that lets the dead tell
their tales to the living: our attempts to sob
in each other's arms futile as turning
back time to before I was called to Troy
by Agamemnon: a second shade, moaning
his wife had slain him for sacrificing
their daughter to gain a fair wind to war.

He and his puling brother Menelaus
stole ten years of my life, killed almost all
of my crew, forced to follow me, their king,
into war. If we few who're left find home,
it will be as beggars fleeing marauders.

When Agamemnon cursed his wife, I wanted
to slash the whining whelp. But to what purpose?
The ghost insubstantial as our glory-dreams:
a whole generation dragged down to death
to retrieve a whore for her cuckold-consort;
and I bereft, Mother among the dead:
grief for my being dragged to Troy killing her.

Would that I'd never left sweet Ithaca
and had no perils to make poems of.
My shipmates' screams will clatter in my ears
like swords smashing shields until I return
to Hades, to dwell in death forever.

Anticlea, Mother of Odysseus, After Her Son Leaves Hades

I could bear my death lightly as the mist
I've been all these years if you hadn't appeared
to disturb my eternal forgetfulness
with memories of my sweet wedding night;
of your birth, your head smudged with blood, bawling,
already impatient to explore the world,

Now that I've been graced with this last sight of you,
how I miss rising to oversee the cook-fires,
the grinding of oats and barley, and helping
my maids slap clothes and sheets clean on river rocks.
How I miss, now, watching you train for war
and raiding: the bringers of wealth and honor.

For in our world, it's raid or be raided.
But when your fleet set sail for thieving Troy,
I stood in the surge with Penelope,
who held small Telemachus in her arms;
we sobbed into his curls, the tide lapping
our knees: sisters in our grief and loss.

After you left, my breath began to rasp;
I'd see wraiths and hold onto the bedpost:
a skiff in rough seas. And when I fainted,
the physic shook his sad head; your father
bowed his, then smiled to show me—the liar—
that there was nothing to worry about.

In death, I had begun to forget you
and everything of the world I had missed.
But now it all comes rushing back to me
like storm waves pounding Ithaca's hard cliffs.
Yes, leave, and take these taunting memories;
give me back precious forgetfulness and peace.

PART VII

—

SAILING PAST THE SIRENS' ROCKS

Leonides, Bard of Ithaca, Asks To Hear the Sirens' Songs

"Lord Odysseus, tie me to the mast
as well, so I can hear their temptress tunes:
my bard's duty to judge their trickery,
their songs that other mortals succumb to,
when the jades play on the longings of men
desperate to see their loved ones and homes.

"I can withstand their lies, as a seer
can read the stars, inspect entrails, or study
falcons and doves, to determine men's fates.
I'll prove I'm more than the match of women
perched on rocks: vultures amid their own shit;
they'll never tempt me to beg for my bonds
to be undone and swim to rocky doom.

"Indeed, leave my hands free to pluck my lyre;
I'll make them weep for their pitiless joy
to coax men to swim to them, to be smashed
on the cliffs that line their treacherous shore.
My songs will shame their lying doggerel.

"Lord Odysseus, I beg you, don't stop
up my ears, for that would cede the battle
to these smirky vixen-faced temptresses.
No, don't take my lyre, nor stop up my mouth:
my only weapons against these witches.
You fighters wield swords, but I've only words
and songs, and my brain that leaps from one phrase
to the next like an ibex on rocky cliffs.

"Thank you, My Lord; I'll make you proud, will pile
honors on the name of Odysseus,
whose bard is the finest in Achaea,
where epics are composed, to please the gods."

*Odysseus Regrets Allowing the Bard Leonides to Listen
to the Sirens' Songs*

Poor fool, filled past the brim with a bard's pride,
and I the stupid agent of his doom
when he insisted I let him listen
to the Sirens' taunting airs and graces.
As his lord, I should've told him to row,
ears wax-stuffed against the Sirens' taunting,
but I wished his melodies to induce
them to swim to our ships, for our sharp swords
to rid these straits of their honeyed venom.

I let him listen, left his hands just free
enough to pluck his lyre; he loosed his bonds,
and dove overboard, hearing nothing save
the Sirens, their words snaking, licking him—
that he'd find the joys of home on their shore,
that they would give him his wife to lie with,
his children to bounce like fearless horsemen
on his knees, that he'd have rest from his toils.

He found boulders sharper than Hector's sword,
harder than the axe that Aeneas wielded,
swifter than Paris' deadly arrows.
Those hideous sisters dove into the surf
churning as if with scores of sharks, to leave
nothing of poor Leonides, not even
his bones for us to bury, as befits
one who honored us all with his poems,
who'd cheered us with drinking-songs between battles,
helped us mourn dead friends with tales of their deeds.

When we finally rowed past that cliff-lair,
I had my men untie me; all we heard,
the slap of waves, the bullwhip-snap of sails.
Then we shipped oars, to weep and remember.

The Sirens, After They Lure Leonides to His Death

We failed, not the bard we wanted, or rather
not just the bard, but this Odysseus,
alleged the cleverest man of the Greeks.
When we saw the singer bound to the mast
along with Odysseus, we intended
for Leonides to untie his chief,
too, not dive into the waves the instant
he heard our songs of smoky nostalgia.

But the fool was feverish as a boy
impatient for his first sword on his name day:
to match dithyrambs with us, immortals.
The undertow alone batted him about
as if orcas battering seals for sport,
the rocks lining the shore like dragon fangs:
dead before he was within a ship-length
of the strand, his lyre shattered to splinters.

Odysseus was still bound to the mast
like cargo secured in a rat-chattering hold.
What pleasure to have watched him drown, mistaking
us for his beloved wife Penelope,
whose voice we imitated perfectly.
How we howled not to be able to coax
him to us, our first inkling of failure.

Some of my sisters wanted to swim out
to their ships and feast on those sailors' flesh,
vengeance, justice for our futile melodies,
but I counseled caution: they may be mortals,
but we've never been tested against swords.

And even divine Aphrodite bled
when she tried to interfere for her beloved
Trojans, when they battled war-mad Argives.

Beliades, After Escaping the Sirens, Remembers
an Ithacan Kitchen Wench

Through the beeswax Odysseus plugged up
my ears with, I heard the hell-maidens taunt
of that kitchen wench we had our way with
on our last night before sailing for Troy
and how she'd stared hatred at us, as hard
as the faces of Trojans, their armor
stripped off, like skinned deer, before they were dead.

Each took turns, and all through it, not a word
from her, nor shriek of pain, though we'd rubbed her
raw and dry as Ithaca's rock-rough shoreline.
When my wife had demanded where I'd been,
I lied, "A strategy meeting with Lord
Odysseus," and before she could prove
me a liar, I took her from behind,
to add the spice of danger to our fucking.

If men are rewarded and fitly punished
for their deeds, I doubt I'll ever behold
sweet Ithaca again. And if I do,
who's to say that scullery slattern hasn't
hissed my treachery to my wife: both bitches
waiting to go at me with nets and spears,
or smiling poison poured into my goblet,
if that kitchen slave hasn't already
cursed me to wander Styx's shore forever.

And what if I made a son on either
of them that last night, and all they'd taught him
was lethal vengeance and not one word of love?

As They Row Past the Sirens, Procris, One of
Odysseus' Crewmen

Even with my ears wax-stuffed, I could hear
them promise if I just swam to their rocks
I'd be with my wife again, make her scream
with pleasure: a wild Maenad's holy trance.
I knew the Sirens were slithery liars,
for I'd never moved my wife to loud joy:
at best, a quick spending, and she scrubbing
my slime off, then going about her chores,
her disappointment carved into her features,
like the quick fizzling of wandering stars.

The night I returned early from our flock—
Tros, my little brother relieving me—
in our hovel, my wife and a kinsman,
her shrieks driving me to plunge my dagger
into his bucking spine, then her belly
in a frenzy I'd never known with her.

I was brought before King Odysseus.
"This is your lucky day, he smiled. "We sail
for Troy with the tide," and me the golden
child of Fate: to dodge my wife's kinsmen's knives.
Ten years later, my punishment's perfect:
always terrified of spears or sword thrusts,
or of waves washing me into the maw
of a giant fish, and now these taunting
bitches, who, Odysseus warned, await
seamen not with warm arms, but with shark fangs.

And if I do return to Ithaca,
memories are long and hard; daggers sharp;
shepherd-nights dark; and the occasional
bleating can dampen an assassin's steps.

For now, I row, hear, through this crumbling wall
of wax, the Sirens' hithering song.
Like all women, they're nothing but liars.

PART VIII

—

BETWEEN SCYLLA AND CHARYBDIS

Threnos, After the Incident with Scylla and Charybdis

I shat myself, as did the other lads
rowing for our terrified lives—to see
those tentacles shoot out from rock-face caves;
this, after the whirlpool Scylla that sucked
two men down its hole to black Tartarus.
When those scaly arms snaked out, Odysseus
shouted, "Pull, pull!" even he shroud-pallid,
men smashed so fast they'd no time to pray.

Those monstrous claws like nothing I've beheld,
or wish to see again, and taking Otos,
who'd saved me time and again at Ilium
when some Trojan had me at his mercy:
a tortoise's stomach exposed to his spear.

Ten years of our lives we gave to that war,
and, after, we'd hoped for a quick row home,
a soft life with wives and kids, begging for tales
on nights of sleet warmed by our hovels' hearths.
I fear, now, we'll never see home: dangers
carving us, except Odysseus, too smart to be killed
by foes, swirling waters, or mere monsters.

After we at last escaped those terrors,
we shipped our oars, drank air, and sobbed for friends,
Otos among them, his wife the finest face
on Ithaca after Penelope—
much good her looks will do him in Hades.

*Otia, the Wife of Otos, at the Moment of Her Husband's Death
from Charybdis*

Strange, I've rarely thought of him, let alone
missed his ponderous weight in my soft bed.
But now, I see his body arced in pain.
He's dead—I sense it—alive all these years,
through all those battles bards chanted of,
other wives enquiring after their husbands;
I knew mine was alive, not that I cared
overmuch, for another, better man
had given me two more boys and a girl
I won't have to tell brazen lies about.

At first, I thought he'd be home with the tide,
a mistake made: war unnecessary,
except some brief and profitable raids.
But after a year, none of our wolf ships
sailed into Ithaca's calm, safe harbor.

So I took Strenos into my hovel,
my bed; he worked hard, at night left me smiling,
while Otos had thrust, grunted, slept atop me
even before his cock stopped pumping juice.
Strenos the one father Praxis has loved,
not knowing Otos from a sack of barley;
and if he returned, Praxis would go at
Otos for a stranger, a usurper.

I'd never have begrudged him a long life
with some other woman who didn't mind
his brute coupling, but no telling what flames
might've roared had he seen me with Strenos.

Otos left bastards on his island raids.
Just like that man to spurn what was offered.
At least he didn't kill those poor women
later, as his shipmates were so fond of doing.

Nexeria, at the Moment of Sensing Her Husband's Death
in the Whirlpool Scylla

Was this why I was chaste for ten years
while the others whose husbands sailed to Troy
took men like cheap robes? When men circled me
like drooling mastiffs, I stayed true to you.
Now, who'll caress my sagging breasts, plunge into
my chasm dry as the steppes east of Troy?
And I'll have you only in fading dreams.

I told you to hide when Odysseus
beat his shield for his vassals to report.
"No one will miss you," I coaxed. "So many
are marching to the harbor like death walkers,
one less corpse will go unnoticed." But you
prattled on about Duty and Honor,
as if those shiftless beggars ever left food
on our table, or warmed our wintry bed.
"Lord Odysseus doesn't even know
who you are," I cajoled, but you strode on.

I refused to kiss you, wave you safely
away, or pray the gods watch over you
as you watched over Odysseus's flocks,
though we all know that sheep are shorn and butchered:
not so different from men thrust into war.

Instead, I cursed at the gods, who avenged
themselves by taking the child inside me.
Now, I'm a wool-spinner too old for the men
who've sprung up on the island since you left.
Still, I hope your end was swift and painless;
I'll pour wine and oil for you, and say prayers,
place a coin where you loved to watch our flocks,
so your soul will be ferried across Styx.

In return, pray to Hades, sweet Persephone,
for a kind, preferably blind older man
for me: recompense for staying faithful
to your memory all these lonely years.

PART IX

—

LOST ON THE BLOOD-DARK SEA

Anakles on the Island of the Sun While Odysseus
Goes Off to Pray

When I beheld the others prepare to feast
on the Sun God's oxen, I begged them not to,
but they were no more fearful of the gods
than that murderous giant Cyclops was
of the law of sacred hospitality.

"Will you snitch on us to Odysseus?"
they taunted, so hungry were they after
our ordeal with Scylla and Charybdis.

Reaching this island, we'd lain gasping, sobbing
for our companions lost in Scylla's eddies
that dragged us down: a beast from Tartarus;
even worse were Charybdis's tentacles
lifting six mates, smashing them on boulders,
devouring them as men enjoy oysters.

Still, before he went to pray, our captain
commanded us to battle our hunger.
"These kine belong to the god, not to us."
But the instant he strode off, my rash mates
butchered the beasts. Though the aromas filled
me with hunger, I refrained from feasting.

When Odysseus beheld the carnage,
he wept, "We're doomed," and ordered us to row,
hoping to outrun the Sun God's vengeance.
But His lightning bolt shattered the mast, tore
up the planks like grass. All were drowned
save Odysseus, clinging to the mast,
while I hugged a plank, drifted, wept, and prayed.

On the third dawn, I spied a sharp shoreline:
Ithaca? The cliffs unmistakable!
Blessing the gods, I gasped on the soft strand
'til I could rise and walk, to find my wife;
then the palace, to inform My Lady
there was still hope for her Lord's homecoming.

Podales, One of Odysseus' Crew Who Feasted
on the Sacred Cattle

Let Odysseus fast; he's a hero,
trained to deny himself and keep going.
But we're mere men dragooned into service,
no desire to follow our Lord to war,
especially one that's lasted ten years.
And what did we get? Some trinkets and coins,
a sword we'd no more use for than an oar
once we're home, since none of us planned to leave.

Troy was bad enough, but so many monsters lurk
on the sea I still tremble from the last ones:
eating our shipmates like succulent plums.

If Odysseus truly wished to keep us
from feasting on the Sun God's oxen,
he'd not have claimed he was going to pray
for our safe return home, but instead stayed with us.

He should have ordered us to raise the sail
and row to Ithaca and our sweet wives,
though I was too young when I was summoned
to possess so fine a creature as a wife;
I was barely old enough to hold a pikestaff.
But I fooled my masters: survived ten years
and deserved a meal for all I'd suffered.

Now our master's returned and is shouting
at us, kicking us, cursing that we're doomed.
"My King," I want to throw back, but don't dare,
"we were doomed the instant we slid bloody
from our dams' wombs: to serve and fight and die
for you, who hardly notice our passing."

*Logomachia, Leader of the Suppliant Women Making Landfall
on the Island of the Sun*

We thought we'd be safe, free from our brute-men
who took pleasure in beating us for not
fetching large dowries, nor having Helen's looks,
for giving them daughters they tossed onto
brambly mountainsides for wolves to devour.
The boys we gave them: nasty as their sires,
our sons slapping us for not bringing meals
quick enough, ordering us like their slaves.
And our men's mothers? Witches who mixed potions
to kill us, after we'd delivered heirs,
no further use for us, we who'd been raised
princess-soft, even if not in great kingdoms.

So we whispered and planned, and one dark night,
snuck to the harbor: death from the sea's fists
preferable to drudgery and rape.
We stole the swiftest ship, made landfall
on the Sun God's island of sacred kine.

But now this Odysseus and his crew
have fetched up, found us hiding, thought to fuck,
then silence us. We all should've come armed,
but only I thought to, so when the beast
who smirked through rotting teeth tried to rip my robe,
I slashed his belly; their laughter stopped,
with his guts pouring out and he toppling.

"Run!" I screamed. Too late, beasts on us, yanking
apart our legs, slitting our throats like sows.
When Charon's raft creaked to Styx's shore, and all
with the coin jostled to board, I herded
my ladies on; despite our empty hands,
the look in my eyes cowed the Ferryman
and the pig I wish I could slay again.

At last we've found rest in Elysium's
soft twilight: without care or toil or men.

Lanx, Dying on the Island of the God of the Sun

After the deaths I'd dodged for endless years
at Troy and on the sea home, I'd a right
to fuck the Sun God's maidens; or whoever
those whores were, cringing from us in a cave.

Just my luck, to pick the slut with a knife,
my guts steaming on the ground, my mates staring
in disbelief, after all those battles,
those monsters and witches, only to die
on this island of women and cattle.

"Lads," I groan, "don't tell my wife how I died.
No need for her to curse me to Tartarus.
As for this bitch, fuck her and slit her throat,
slit all their throats, bury them all before
Odysseus returns from his prayers."

Now, I stand on Styx's shore, crowds of the dead
pleading. The slut who did for me here too,
her sneer wide as a scar made by boar tusks.
If we weren't shades, she'd rip my eyes out;
I'd snap her neck: a fox in the hen house.

But I gloat: me with the coin, her without;
so let her stand here like the Queen of Hades,
forever: she won't get across and I will.

But when I hand my coin to the Ferryman,
this bold bitch follows me onto his raft
as if she owns it, and Charon lets her!
Worse than Tartarus, to spend eternity
in blessed Elysium with this whore.

Pelaxes, About to Drown in the Typhoon

We're punished with death by the pummeling
sea because we feasted on the Sun God's
kine? Yes, more likely for the devoured herd
than for the harridans we found and fucked:
too long since we'd felt women's slick thighs,
and our lord said nothing about those whores
being sacred to the god, like the cattle.
Maybe Odysseus knew nothing of them:
escaped from raiders, only to fall to us.

One dagger-slashed Lanx, his guts spilling out.
I yanked the blade away, and fought her fists,
her teeth trying to rake my face, until
I smacked her like that half-god, Heracles.
After that, she gave me no more trouble.
But far, far too long since we'd been allowed
at the strumpets, so I blame the gods:
for placing temptation in our hard way.

Who could've resisted the whores? Gorgeous,
skin the cream of new milk and twice as hot.
They may have shrieked, "No!" but they were willing,
all but my whore: the bitch with the dagger,
hot in her rage, twice as hot as all the others.

To ensure Odysseus wouldn't find out,
we buried them in a part of the woods
we knew he'd not be walking back from after
he'd prayed to the god and asked for His help
in finding the easiest sea road home.

Home? Tartarus. But they were mere women,
thus put here to serve the whims of heroes.

Traxeleus, Another of Odysseus' Shipmates, About to Drown

Anakles warned us that to eat the cattle
of the Sun and to pollute and murder
those hiding women was a sacrilege:
their island, after all, or suppliants,
not prey to be taken as owls dig talons
into the spines of terrified field mice.

We assured him, "The whores'll be eager
as she-wolves in heat" and laughed at the man,
prim as a spinster, not a warrior.

When that one woman, taller than the rest,
slashed Lanx—his guts spilling like smoking soup
from a boiling cauldron—we stood frozen
a moment, then went at them like wild dogs.
After we'd secretly buried the whores,
we butchered the cattle, feasted, drank wine
and more wine, and at last slept, dreamt of our wives,

only to waken when Odysseus
returned from praying for our safe voyage home.
Shouting, "What have you fools done?" he beat us
and ordered, "Put your backs into your oars!
No sails to ease your toil, you pack of jackals!
The god knows what filth you've all committed.
Now row, you bastards, for your scummy lives!"

The typhoon hit like a thousand Trojan spears;
waves higher than the walls of Troy, higher
than the shafts Odysseus shot from the bow
only he could draw to its full tension:
waves like the outraged fists of great Ajax,
waves smothering me in their frozen arms,
dragging me to Tartarus, where I belong.

PART X

—

ODYSSEUS SITS DOWN TO WEEP

Wandering the Shore of Calypso's Island, Odysseus
Sits Down to Weep

Gone, all my shipmates gone, the men I sailed
to Troy with, the men I braved the brutish
seas back to Ithaca with: eaten by
the Cyclops; smashed by monstrous Laestrygons;
turned into swine by witch-Circe; sucked down
Scylla's maw or snatched by Charybdis'
tentacles, splattered on rocks, and devoured.

I thought once we'd made our tearful landfall
on the Island of the Sun and I'd warned them
not to feast on the god's sacred cattle
while I went to pray for a good west wind,
it would be a quick pull for Ithaca.

But they defied my orders and were drowned,
I alone washing up on this island
I've no heart to explore, to find other
mortals: harmless, or fearsome as the monsters
only I escaped: naked, battered by waves.

In the distance, a woman flutters more
than walks, as if a film of fire. No doubt
a goddess. Another Circe, bent on
turning me into a pig for her feast?
Or perhaps her immortal heart can pity
a mere man's troubles, and she'll send me home.

No use hiding: in a blink, she's beside me.
Exhausted, despairing from the sea, I rasp

"I am Odysseus, the last Ithacan
left after years of war and the blood-dark sea."

She smiles, bids me follow; whether to doom
or undreamt joys, I've no will to refuse,
when all I want is my wife's love-warm arms
and to rest my weary head, and to sleep.

Dolmedes Also Makes Landfall on the Island of Calypso

I have no idea why I, of all those
who sinned by eating the Sun God's oxen,
was spared. Maybe it's because I refrained
from despoiling and murdering those poor women:
our dreadful feast sacrilege enough.
In any case, I clung to planks and prayed.
But, oh, it was a weary, weary drifting,
landing on one island after another,
each more arid, each with less sustenance;
but I kept going, hoping the next islet
might be Ithaca, or at least populated
by folk who didn't feast on humans,
years piling on like rocks at a cliff's base.

Finally, I lay gasping on this strand
and, standing over me, Odysseus,
my captain, my king; and beside him,
a smiling goddess, Calypso; so splendid
was she, I could stare at her forever.

"You've been drifting for a long time," she spoke,
musical as an expertly plucked lyre.
"Come, eat, rest—we'll talk after you're refreshed."

The next dawn, Odysseus led me back
to the strand; staring out to sea, he sighed,
"You can do me a great kindness," and eyed
my raft, testing its vines and sturdy planks.
"Trade your craft for this island paradise.
The goddess has agreed; your life will be soft,
no more terrors on the sea. No more aging,
as we've both done—our hair woven with gray."

I'd no courage to face the sea again,
no guarantee I'd ever embrace my wife;
that my now-grown sons wouldn't kill me,
taking me for a scheming interloper.

Besides, the goddess seemed amenable.
even if I wasn't of royal blood.

"You will more than suffice," she smiled, seeing
my weary soul, then led me to her palace,
Odysseus slipping away, while she
took me in hand, the wind perfect for sailing.

The Goddess Calypso Ponders Her New Companion,
Dolmedes

After I let bright Odysseus sail
for Ithaca—I granted his proxy
eternal life. When he sees he'll never die,
never age, he'll never leave: how can he
marry a mortal, knowing long after
she's dust, he'll still be a man in life's prime,
grieving forever at Time's betrayal.

Unbearable were my eons alone
before Odysseus, the solitude
deeper than the snows of Ultima Thule.
And when he fetched up on my shore—
beaten by the waves like a giant's fists—
I thought, "At last, my mate!" But he was so
heartbroken for his wife, I grew weary
of his pining for her, whom he forsook
for this Troy mortals laud as their great war.

A wrist flick and I'd destroy both armies.
Still, I envy that they can die, lending
savor to their lives, the gift of surviving
dangers I'll never know: eternal life
slothful: a finger-snap brings ambrosia.

Finally, I told him if I could find
a suitable replacement, he could leave.
Dolmedes fetched up on my strand. He's not
of noble birth, but handsome, and speaks well,
and listens with a true smile of delight
when I play the lyre, and takes me lion-fierce.

To keep him from boredom, I'll make monsters
for him to slay, marauders to fight off.
Meanwhile, he revels in immortality
like a small boy given his first true sword.

EPILOGUE

Safely Home on Ithaca, Odysseus Remembers
His Lost Companions

We were as good as the gods let us be,
no worse than other men who went to war:
caught by war-madness and the blood-dark sea

that drowned us in despair onto our knees,
quaking like rabbits to see our own gore
ripped by monsters who never let us be.

Still, we provoked our dooms, in honesty:
on our raids of peaceful, husbanded shores;
we were war-mad at Troy and on the sea.

But let me toast you all: Lykanos, free
and powerful when you pulled at your oar;
you were as good as the gods let you be.

And Procris, cursed by your wife's bitchery
with her kinsman; and you, dear Elpenor,
war-mad, then lost beside the blood-dark sea

when you were ensnared by the witch, Circe,
and shoved from her roof by one of her whores.
All my men: good as the gods let you be,
caught in war's madness and the death-dark sea.

Acknowledgments

The author gratefully acknowledges the following journals in which the poems listed below, some in earlier form, first appeared:

Blue Unicorn: "Wandering the Shore of Calypso's Island, Odysseus Sits Down to Weep"

Cairn: "Lykanos, Rowing Safely Away from the Coast of Ismarus"

Classical Outlook: "Odysseus Leaves Troy," "Xenios Finds a Way to Escape Troy," "Elpenor, Rowing from Troy, Under Odysseus' Command," "Menardes Remains Among the Lotos Eaters," "Meliades, Dying at the Hands of the Cicones, on Ismarus," "Temnios Escapes the Land of the Cicones," "Cowering in Polyphemos' Cave, Meres Remembers His Brother Axatilles, the First Ithacan Killed at Troy," "Straygos, As They Drop Anchor Outside the Harbor of the Laestrygons," "Sailing from the Cyclops, Odysseus Apologizes to His Crew," "Odysseus, After His Apology to His Crew," "Anticlea, Mother of Odysseus, After Her Son Leaves Hades"

Ekphrasis: "Licius Remains Among the Lotos Eaters," "Odysseus, After His Visit to Hades," The Goddess Calypso Ponders Her New Companion, Dolmedes"

The New Orphic Review (Canada): "The Myrmidon Letheres, a Stowaway on Odysseus' Flagship," "The Lotos Eaters Begin to Complain About the Presence of Odysseus and His Shipmates," "Leonides, Bard of Ithaca, Escapes the Cyclops," "Polymenes Opens the Bag of Winds to Disastrous Consequences," "Xanthos Considers His Friend Polymenes As they Row Away from the Land of the Laestrygons," "Selax, Turned into a Leopard by Circe," "Odysseus Regrets Allowing the Bard Leonides Listen to the Sirens' Songs"

The Sewanee Review: "Anakles on the Island of the Sun While Odysseus Goes Off to Pray," "Podales, One of Odysseus' Crew Who Feasted on the Sacred Cattle"

About FutureCycle Press

FutureCycle Press is dedicated to publishing lasting English-language poetry books, chapbooks, and anthologies in both print-on-demand and Kindle ebook formats. Founded in 2007 by long-time independent editor/publishers and partners Diane Kistner and Robert S. King, the press incorporated as a nonprofit in 2012. A number of our editors are distinguished poets and writers in their own right, and we have been actively involved in the small press movement going back to the early seventies.

The FutureCycle Poetry Book Prize and honorarium is awarded annually for the best full-length volume of poetry we publish in a calendar year. Introduced in 2013, our Good Works projects are anthologies devoted to issues of universal significance, with all proceeds donated to a related worthy cause. Our Selected Poems series highlights contemporary poets with a substantial body of work to their credit; with this series we strive to resurrect work that has had limited distribution and is now out of print.

We are dedicated to giving all of the authors we publish the care their work deserves, making our catalog of titles the most diverse and distinguished it can be, and paying forward any earnings to fund more great books.

We've learned a few things about independent publishing over the years. We've also evolved a unique, resilient publishing model that allows us to focus mainly on vetting and preserving for posterity poetry collections of exceptional quality without becoming overwhelmed with bookkeeping and mailing, fundraising activities, or taxing editorial and production "bubbles." To find out more about what we are doing, come see us at www.futurecycle.org.

The FutureCycle Poetry Book Prize

All full-length volumes of poetry published by FutureCycle Press in a given calendar year are considered for the annual FutureCycle Poetry Book Prize. This allows us to consider each submission on its own merits, outside of the context of a contest. Too, the judges see the finished book, which will have benefitted from the beautiful book design and strong editorial gloss we are famous for.

The book ranked the best in judging is announced as the prize-winner in the subsequent year. There is no fixed monetary award; instead, the winning poet receives an honorarium of 20% of the total net royalties from all poetry books and chapbooks the press sold online in the year the winning book was published. The winner is also accorded the honor of being on the panel of judges for the next year's competition; all judges receive copies of all contending books to keep for their personal library.

www.ingramcontent.com/pod-product-compliance
Lightning Source LLC
Chambersburg PA
CBHW070005100426
42741CB00012B/3117